W9-AUD-659

Extreme Cuisine
Spider-tizers
and Other
Creepy Treats

by Meish Goldish

Consultants:
David George Gordon, author of *The Eat-a-Bug Cookbook*
Andrew Zimmern, co-creator and host of *Bizarre Foods with Andrew Zimmern*

BEARPORT
PUBLISHING

New York, New York

Credits

Cover and Title Page, © John Bell/Shutterstock and Robyn MacKenzie/Shutterstock; 4, © James Carmichael Jr./NHPA/Photoshot; 5, © Owen Franken/Corbis; 6, © Randy May; 7, © Robert James Elliott/OnAsia.com; 8, © John Mitchell/Oxford Scientific/Photolibrary; 9, © Peter Menzel/from the book "Man Eating Bugs"/www.menzelphoto.com; 10, © Jeff Hill/Dreamstime; 11, © Ken Lambert/The Seattle Times; 12, © Dan O'Flynn/Alamy; 13, © Robert Ross Gallo Images/Photodisc/Alamy; 14L, © Kim Taylor/Dorling Kindersley/Getty Images; 14R, © Ceerwan Aziz/Reuters/Landov; 15, © Yang Xi/UPPA/Photoshot; 16, © blickwinkel/fotototo/Alamy; 17, © Michael Freeman; 18, © Peter Parks/AFP/Getty Images; 19, © Peter Menzel/from the book "Man Eating Bugs"/www.menzelphoto.com; 20T, © Peter Menzel/from the book "Man Eating Bugs"/www.menzelphoto.com; 20B, © Dorling Kindersley/Getty Images; 21, © Yoong Wearn Lim; 23TL, © Judy Tejero/Shutterstock; 23TR, © Andrejs Jegorovs/Shutterstock; 23C, © John Bell/Shutterstock; 23BR, © Terese Loeb Kreuzer/Alamy; 23BL, © Olga Lyubkina/Shutterstock; 24, © Eric Isselée/Shutterstock.

Publisher: Kenn Goin
Editorial Director: Adam Siegel
Creative Director: Spencer Brinker
Design: Debrah Kaiser
Photo Researcher: Laura Saravia

Library of Congress Cataloging-in-Publication Data

Goldish, Meish.
  Spider-tizers and other creepy treats / by Meish Goldish.
     p. cm. — (Extreme cuisine)
  Includes bibliographical references and index.
  ISBN-13: 978-1-59716-759-8 (lib. binding)
  ISBN-10: 1-59716-759-2 (lib. binding)
  1. Cookery (Insects)—Juvenile literature. 2. Spiders—Juvenile literature. 3. Cookery, International—Juvenile literature. I. Title.

  TX746.G655 2009
  641.6'96—dc22

                                      2008038279

For more information, write to Bearport Publishing Company, Inc., 101 Fifth Avenue, Suite 6R, New York, New York 10003. Printed in the United States of America.

10 9 8 7 6 5 4 3 2 1

~ MENU ~

Spider Starters

Some meals begin with an **appetizer**, such as cheese and crackers or chips and dip. It makes a person hungry for more food. How about a spider to start a meal? Why not? These eight-legged creatures are eaten all over the world.

In parts of northern Thailand, some people hunt and cook tarantulas. They are some of the hairiest—and biggest—spiders in the world. Before cooking them, villagers pull off the spiders' legs. Then they roast the bodies and eat them. In Bangkok, the capital of Thailand, some people fry tarantulas and serve them on top of noodles. Of course, not everyone is ready for a big spider meal. Some people might want to start with just one tarantula—the perfect "spider-tizer."

tarantula

fried tarantula

Spiders are a good source of protein, which a person's body needs to build and repair bone and muscle.

Deep-Fried Spiders

In parts of Cambodia, tarantulas are a popular snack. Some people even sell them in the street. On a good day, a person can sell 100 to 200 tarantulas. Where do the street vendors get their spiders? People dig the hairy creatures out of their underground homes, called **burrows**. A skillful hunter can catch more than 200 spiders in one day.

How are the tarantulas cooked? The hairy spiders are deep-fried in oil with garlic and salt. They're crispy on the outside and soft on the inside. Just be careful when eating them. After munching on a few, some people have found little spider fur balls in their throats.

tarantula

deep-fried tarantulas

A tarantula's head and body have white meat that tastes like a combination of chicken and fish.

Giant Spider Dish

The biggest spider in the world is the goliath birdeater tarantula. With its legs spread out, it is about 11 inches (28 cm) long. That's as big as some dinner plates. Yet the goliath birdeater isn't just a huge spider. It can also be a big meal.

In Venezuela, the Piaroa (pee-uh-ROH-uh) Indians catch the spiders and roast them over hot coals. Some say the meat tastes like shrimp or crab. Very little of the spider's body is wasted. Before eating the eight-legged creature, the Piaroa remove the spider's **fangs**. They will use them as toothpicks after the tasty meal has been eaten.

The goliath birdeater tarantula got its name because it sometimes eats baby birds.

goliath birdeater tarantula

bird

9

Tarantula Tempura

In Japan, vegetables and seafood are often dipped in batter and fried in hot oil. The light, crispy food is called tempura (tem-POOR-uh). Cooks in the United States also make tempura, though not always with the same ingredients. Instead of vegetables or seafood, they sometimes fry spiders!

To make tarantula tempura, a cook cuts off the back part of the spider's body, called the abdomen. Then the creature's hairs are burned off using matches or a lighter. The hairless spider is dipped in tempura batter and fried in oil for about three minutes. After cooking, the legs are cut off and placed on a plate. Eight crispy treats are now ready to be eaten.

abdomen

tarantula tempura

In China and other parts of Asia, some people use spiders to make medicines.

Raw Spiders

Tarantulas aren't the only spiders that people eat. In Laos (LAH-ohs), the golden orb web spider makes a tasty meal. Some people bite off the spider's abdomen and eat it raw. Others cook the spider first and then dip it in salt. They, too, eat only the abdomen. People say it tastes like raw potato mixed with lettuce.

golden orb web spider

abdomen

On the island of New Guinea, people cook golden orb web spiders over a fire. The roasted spiders taste like peanut butter, only not as thick.

golden orb web spider

Centipede Kebabs

People on the go often grab a slice of pizza or buy a hot dog from a **pushcart**. Sometimes they buy kebabs—grilled pieces of meat on a **skewer**. They're a quick and easy way to have lunch without taking the time to sit down.

In Beijing (BAY-JING), the capital of China, people in a rush can snack on centipede kebabs. The leggy creatures are placed on wooden skewers and then fried. They have a crunchy outside and a gooey center. Watch out for the sharp legs, though. They can get stuck on a person's lips.

centipede

seahorse kebabs

Other animals in China that are cooked and sold on skewers include seahorses and scorpions.

15

Fried Scorpions

Scorpions and spiders belong to a large group of animals called arachnids (uh-RAK-nidz). Both kinds of creatures have eight legs—and they can both make a tasty meal.

A restaurant in Singapore serves fried scorpions. They are placed on top of pumpernickel bread along with red or yellow pepper and boiled asparagus. The crispy creatures are so delicious they are eaten whole—including the claws and tail.

stinger

scorpion

A scorpion has a poisonous stinger on the end of its tail. Don't worry about eating it, however. Once the scorpion is cooked, the poison becomes harmless.

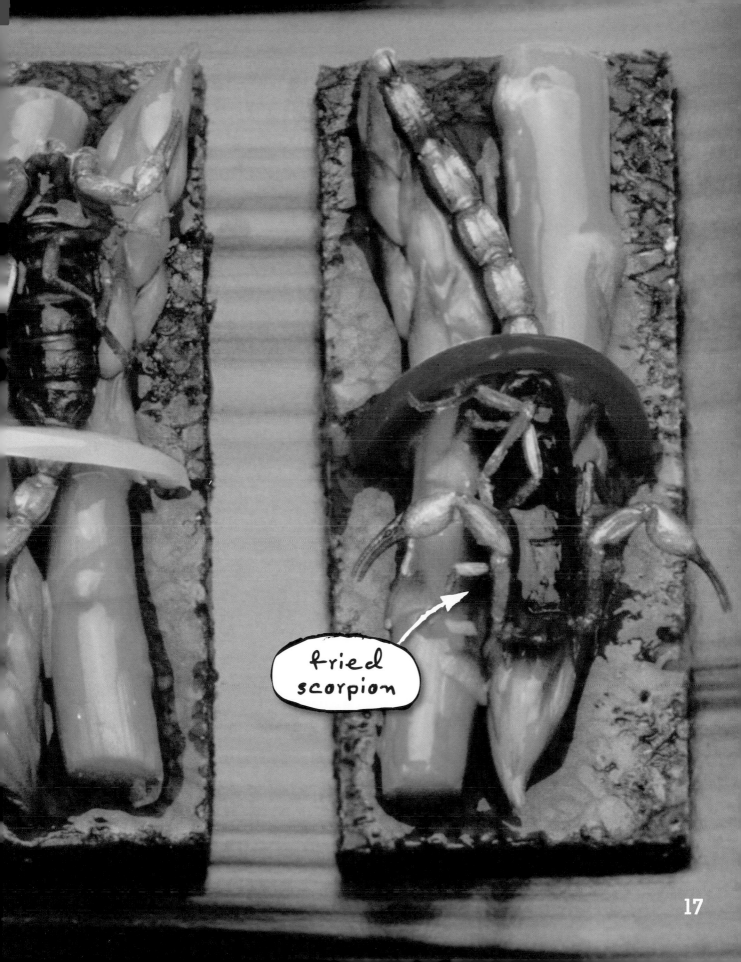

fried scorpion

Scorpion Soup

Scorpions can be eaten in many ways. Some people in China eat them raw. The poisonous stingers must be removed first, however, so the animal is safe to eat. Other people in China use scorpions to make soup. To make the dish, the cook first washes 30 to 40 live scorpions. Then the creatures are stir-fried with pork, garlic, ginger, salt, and pepper. Next, the cook adds water, dates, and carrots. Finally, it's all heated on a low flame for about 40 minutes.

Scorpions are so popular in China that the stinging animals are raised and sold for food. One company alone raises three million scorpions at a time!

It's dangerous to hold a live scorpion. While its sting is rarely strong enough to kill a person, the poison can cause painful swelling and fever.

scorpions

scorpion soup

Candy Scorpions and Spiders

Most Americans won't eat a scorpion—even after it's turned into candy. Still, some companies are trying to change people's minds. How? They are making scorpions dipped in chocolate and lollipops with real scorpions inside. The scorpion suckers come in many flavors, including blueberry, banana, apple, and strawberry.

Many kids eat gummy spiders, but they're not made with real spiders—at least not yet. If Americans enjoy licking scorpion lollipops, perhaps someday they'll like snacking on sweet spiders as well.

scorpion dipped in chocolate

gummy spiders

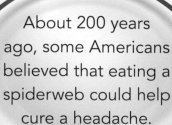

About 200 years ago, some Americans believed that eating a spiderweb could help cure a headache.

Where Are They Eaten?

Here are some of the places where spider, centipede, and scorpion dishes are eaten.

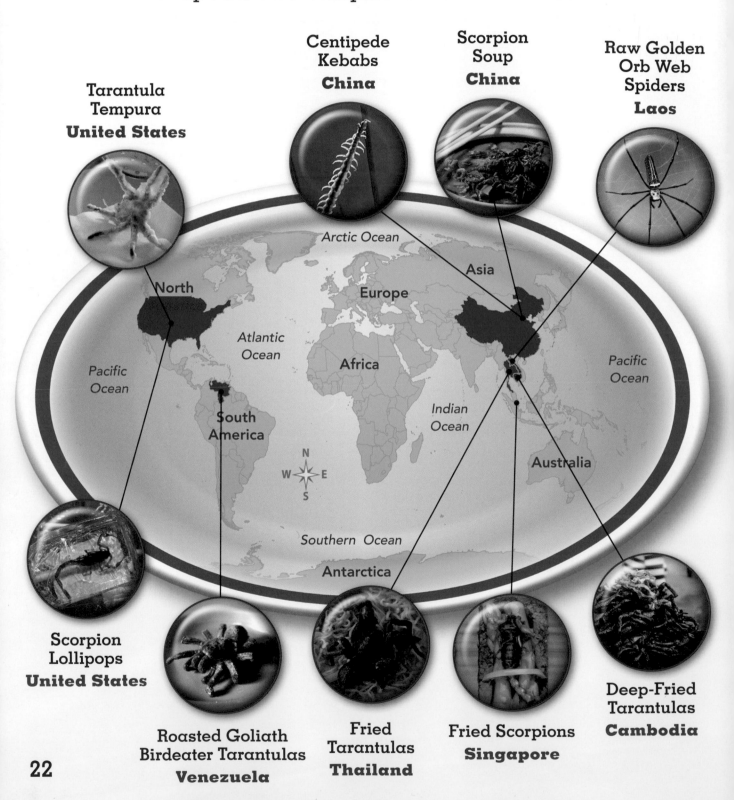

Tarantula
Tempura
United States

Centipede
Kebabs
China

Scorpion
Soup
China

Raw Golden
Orb Web
Spiders
Laos

Arctic Ocean

Asia

Europe

North

Atlantic
Ocean

Africa

Pacific
Ocean

Pacific
Ocean

South
America

Indian
Ocean

Australia

N
W E
S

Southern Ocean

Antarctica

Scorpion
Lollipops
United States

Roasted Goliath
Birdeater Tarantulas
Venezuela

Fried
Tarantulas
Thailand

Fried Scorpions
Singapore

Deep-Fried
Tarantulas
Cambodia

Glossary

appetizer (AP-uh-*tye*-zur)
a small amount of food
eaten before the main meal
that is meant to make a
person hungry for more food

burrows (BUR-ohz)
holes or tunnels in
the ground made by
animals for them to
live in

fangs (FANGZ)
sharp, hollow parts of
a spider's mouth that
can inject poison

pushcart (PUSH-kart)
a cart that is pushed
by hand and is used
by people to sell their
goods on the street

skewer (SKYOO-ur)
a long, thin piece of metal
or wood used to hold meat
and vegetables while
they are being cooked

Index

Bibliography

Gordon, David George. *The Eat-a-Bug Cookbook: 33 Ways to Cook Grasshoppers, Ants, Water Bugs, Spiders, Centipedes, and Their Kin.* Berkeley, CA: Ten Speed Press (1998).

Hopkins, Jerry. *Extreme Cuisine: The Weird & Wonderful Foods That People Eat.* London: Bloomsbury (2004).

Menzel, Peter, and Faith D'Aluisio. *Man Eating Bugs: The Art and Science of Eating Insects.* Berkeley, CA: Ten Speed Press (1998).

Read More

Masoff, Joy. *Oh, Yuck!: The Encyclopedia of Everything Nasty.* New York: Workman (2000).

Solheim, James. *It's Disgusting and We Ate It!: True Food Facts from Around the World and Throughout History.* New York: Simon & Schuster (2001).

Learn More Online

To learn more about spider, scorpion, and centipede dishes, visit **www.bearportpublishing.com/ExtremeCuisine**

About the Author

Meish Goldish has written more than 100 books for children. He lives in Brooklyn, New York. He has never eaten a spider or a scorpion.